FROM HEARTBREAK TO HEALING

Get the support and guidance you need to navigate the Healing process, rebuild intimacy, restore your self-worth, and move forward with hope and confidence

GENEVIEVE STEELE

Table of contents

Introduction

In the journey from heartbreak to healing, there's a crucial need for support, guidance, and understanding. This book serves as a beacon of light for those traversing this challenging path, offering insights, tools, and hope for rebuilding a fulfilling life. Through these pages, readers will find solace in knowing that they are not alone in their struggles and that healing is not just possible but achievable.

Welcome Message

To every reader embarking on this transformative journey, welcome. Whether you've recently experienced heartbreak or are still grappling with its aftermath, know that you've taken a courageous step towards healing. Within these pages, you'll find not only validation for your emotions but also practical strategies to navigate through the pain and emerge stronger on the other side. Your healing journey starts here, and I'm honored to accompany you through it.

How to Use This Book

Navigating a book on healing can sometimes feel overwhelming, especially when emotions are raw. That's why this section is dedicated to guiding you through the contents and making the most of your reading experience. Begin by familiarizing yourself with the table of contents, which provides a roadmap of the chapters ahead. Each chapter is designed to address specific aspects of the healing journey, from understanding heartbreak to restoring self-worth and moving forward with confidence.

As you delve into each chapter, take your time to absorb the material. Pause when needed to reflect on how the concepts resonate with your own experiences. You may find it helpful to journal your thoughts and emotions as you progress, allowing for deeper self-discovery and insight. Additionally, don't hesitate to revisit sections that feel particularly relevant or challenging. Healing is a nonlinear process, and it's okay to take things at your own pace.

Throughout the book, you'll encounter practical exercises, reflective prompts, and real-life stories to illustrate key concepts. These interactive elements are designed to enhance your learning experience and provide tangible tools for personal growth. Remember, healing is not just about absorbing information but also actively engaging with it and applying it to your own life.

Above all, approach this book with an open heart and a willingness to embrace change. Healing is a journey of self-discovery and transformation, and by embarking on it, you've already taken a significant step towards reclaiming your inner strength and resilience. Trust in the process, lean on the support offered within these pages, and know that brighter days lie ahead.

Chapter 1

Understanding Heartbreak

What is Heartbreak?

Heartbreak is a profound emotional experience characterized by intense feelings of sadness, grief, and loss following the end of a significant relationship or the betrayal of trust. It transcends mere sadness; it's a visceral ache that permeates every aspect of one's being. It's the shattered dreams, the broken promises, and the sudden realization that the future once envisioned will never come to pass. Heartbreak can be triggered by various circumstances, such as the dissolution of a romantic partnership, the death of a loved one, or the rupture of a close friendship. Regardless of the cause, the

pain of heartbreak is universal, transcending age, gender, and cultural background.

At its core, heartbreak represents the unraveling of the emotional bond that once connected two individuals. It's the disintegration of trust, intimacy, and mutual understanding that leaves behind a void filled with unanswered questions and unresolved emotions. In essence, heartbreak is a form of grief, akin to mourning the loss of a loved one. Just as in bereavement, those experiencing heartbreak may cycle through stages of denial, anger, bargaining, depression, and eventually, acceptance. Each stage brings its own challenges and complexities, further complicating the healing process.

The Impact of Heartbreak on Mental Health

The ramifications of heartbreak extend far beyond the realm of emotions, profoundly impacting one's mental health and overall well-being. The emotional turmoil accompanying heartbreak can trigger a cascade of psychological symptoms, ranging from profound sadness and despair to anxiety, insomnia, and even clinical depression. The intensity and duration of these symptoms may vary depending on factors such as the nature of the relationship, the circumstances surrounding the breakup, and the individual's coping mechanisms.

One of the most significant psychological consequences of heartbreak is a pervasive sense of worthlessness and self-doubt. Individuals may internalize the rejection or betrayal experienced during the breakup, leading to a profound erosion of self-esteem and self-confidence. This negative self-perception can fuel a vicious cycle of rumination and self-blame, exacerbating feelings of despair and hopelessness.

Moreover, heartbreak can disrupt one's sense of identity and purpose, leaving them adrift in a sea of uncertainty and existential questioning. The loss of a significant relationship can shatter the foundation upon which one's sense of self was built, forcing them to reevaluate their beliefs, values, and life goals. This existential crisis can be both disorienting and disconcerting, further exacerbating feelings of anxiety and depression.

In addition to its psychological toll, heartbreak can also manifest in physical symptoms, such as fatigue, headaches, and gastrointestinal distress. The mind-body connection is a powerful force, and the emotional upheaval of heartbreak can manifest in a myriad of somatic complaints. These physical symptoms serve as a tangible reminder of the profound impact of heartbreak on one's overall well-being.

Recognizing Signs of Heartbreak

Recognizing the signs of heartbreak is the first step towards acknowledging and addressing its impact on one's life. While the experience of heartbreak is highly individualized, there are common emotional, behavioral, and physical indicators that may signal its presence. Emotionally, individuals experiencing heartbreak may exhibit symptoms of profound sadness, tearfulness, irritability, and mood swings. They may struggle to find joy in activities they once enjoyed and may withdraw from social interactions.

Behaviorally, those experiencing heartbreak may engage in coping mechanisms such as excessive alcohol or substance use, overeating or undereating, and reckless behavior. These maladaptive coping strategies serve as temporary distractions from the pain of heartbreak but ultimately exacerbate the emotional turmoil.

Physically, heartbreak can manifest in a variety of somatic symptoms, including fatigue, headaches, muscle tension, and gastrointestinal distress. These physical manifestations serve as tangible reminders of the profound impact of heartbreak on one's overall well-being.

Recognizing these signs is the first step towards acknowledging and validating one's experience of heartbreak. By acknowledging the presence of heartbreak and seeking support, individuals can begin the journey towards healing and restoration.

Chapter 2

Navigating the Healing Process

Navigating the healing process after experiencing heartbreak is a journey that requires courage, resilience, and self-compassion. It's a journey of self-discovery and transformation, where individuals learn to navigate the complex landscape of their emotions and reclaim their sense of agency and purpose. In this chapter, I'll explore three essential components of the healing process: accepting your feelings, coping strategies for healing, and seeking professional help.

Accepting Your Feelings

One of the first steps towards healing from heartbreak is acknowledging and accepting the full range of emotions that accompany the experience. It's natural to feel a whirlwind of conflicting emotions, including sadness, anger, confusion, and even relief. These emotions may come in waves, ebbing and flowing unpredictably as you navigate the ups and downs of the healing journey. Rather than suppressing or denying these feelings, it's essential to allow yourself to fully experience them without judgment or self-criticism.

Acceptance doesn't mean resignation or passivity; it's about acknowledging the reality of your emotions and giving yourself permission to feel them deeply. This process of emotional acceptance can be both liberating and empowering, allowing you to cultivate a greater sense of self-awareness and emotional resilience. By honoring your feelings and allowing them to surface, you create space for healing and growth to occur.

One effective technique for accepting your feelings is mindfulness meditation, which involves observing your thoughts and emotions without attachment or judgment. By practicing mindfulness, you can develop a greater sense of presence and self-compassion, allowing you to navigate the challenges of heartbreak with greater ease and clarity. Additionally, journaling can be a powerful tool for processing and expressing your emotions safely and constructively.

Coping Strategies for Healing

In addition to accepting your feelings, it's essential to develop healthy coping strategies to navigate the healing process effectively. Coping strategies are tools and techniques that help you manage stress, regulate emotions, and cultivate resilience in the face of adversity. While there's no one-size-fits-all approach to coping with heartbreak, there are several evidence-based strategies that have been shown to be effective in promoting healing and well-being.

One such strategy is self-care, which involves prioritizing your physical, emotional, and spiritual well-being. This may include engaging in activities that bring you joy and relaxation, such as exercise, spending time in nature, practicing hobbies, or connecting with supportive friends and family members. Self-care also involves setting boundaries and saying no to activities or commitments that drain your energy or exacerbate stress.

Another essential coping strategy is cognitive restructuring, which involves challenging and reframing negative thought patterns associated with heartbreak. This may involve identifying and challenging irrational beliefs, such as "I'll never find love again" or "I'm not worthy of happiness." By replacing these negative beliefs with more balanced and realistic thoughts, you can cultivate a more positive and compassionate mindset.

Additionally, engaging in activities that promote self-expression and creativity, such as art therapy, writing, or music, can be powerful tools for processing and expressing your emotions. These creative outlets provide a safe and non-judgmental space to explore your feelings and gain insight into your inner world.

Finally, practicing relaxation techniques such as deep breathing, progressive muscle relaxation, or guided imagery can help alleviate stress and promote a sense of calm and relaxation. These techniques activate the body's relaxation response, counteracting the physiological effects of stress and promoting physical and emotional well-being.

Seeking Professional Help

While self-care strategies can be powerful tools for promoting healing, there may be times when professional support is needed to navigate the complexities of heartbreak. Seeking the guidance of a qualified therapist or counselor can provide valuable insights, support, and coping strategies to facilitate the healing process.

Therapy offers a safe and confidential space to explore your thoughts, feelings, and experiences in-depth, allowing you to gain a deeper understanding of yourself and your relationships. A therapist can help you identify and challenge negative thought patterns, develop healthy coping skills, and explore underlying issues that may be contributing to your emotional distress.

In addition to traditional talk therapy, there are several evidence-based approaches that may be helpful for individuals healing from heartbreak. For example, cognitive-behavioral therapy (CBT) focuses on identifying and challenging maladaptive thought patterns and behaviors, while dialectical behavior therapy (DBT) emphasizes mindfulness, emotion regulation, and interpersonal effectiveness skills.

Furthermore, support groups can provide a sense of community and validation for individuals navigating similar experiences of heartbreak. Whether in-person or online, support groups offer an opportunity to connect with others who understand and empathize with your struggles, reducing feelings of isolation and loneliness.

Overall, seeking professional help is a proactive step towards healing and reclaiming your sense of well-being after experiencing heartbreak. A therapist or counselor can provide the guidance, support, and resources you need to navigate the healing process effectively and emerge stronger and more resilient on the other side.

Chapter 3

Rebuilding Intimacy

Rebuilding intimacy after experiencing heartbreak is a delicate yet transformative process that involves reconnecting with oneself and nurturing the bonds with a partner. Intimacy encompasses emotional, physical, and spiritual connection, and rebuilding it requires vulnerability, honesty, and commitment. In this chapter, I'll explore three essential components of rebuilding intimacy: reconnecting with yourself, communicating with your partner, and engaging in intimacy-building exercises.

Reconnecting with Yourself

Before you can fully connect with a partner, it's essential to first reconnect with yourself on a deep and authentic level. Heartbreak can leave you feeling fragmented and disconnected from your innermost thoughts, feelings, and desires. Reconnecting with yourself involves engaging in self-reflection, self-compassion, and self-discovery to cultivate a deeper sense of self-awareness and self-love.

One powerful way to reconnect with yourself is through practices such as mindfulness meditation, yoga, or journaling. These practices help you quiet the noise of the outside world and tune into your inner voice, allowing you to explore your thoughts, feelings, and values with greater clarity and compassion. By cultivating a regular mindfulness practice, you can develop a greater sense of presence and acceptance, enabling you to navigate the complexities of your inner landscape with grace and resilience.

Additionally, engaging in activities that bring you joy and fulfillment, such as pursuing hobbies, spending time in nature, or connecting with supportive friends, can help you rediscover the essence of who you are outside of your past relationships. These activities provide a sense of purpose and meaning, fostering a deeper connection with yourself and enhancing your overall well-being.

Self-care is another essential component of reconnecting with yourself. Prioritizing your physical, emotional, and spiritual well-being through practices such as exercise, proper nutrition, adequate sleep, and relaxation techniques is crucial for replenishing your energy and fostering a sense of inner balance and harmony. By taking care of yourself, you signal to yourself and others that you are worthy of love, respect, and attention.

Communicating with Your Partner

Effective communication is the cornerstone of a healthy and fulfilling relationship, especially in the aftermath of heartbreak. Open, honest, and compassionate communication allows you and your partner to express your thoughts, feelings, and needs openly and authentically, fostering a deeper sense of connection and understanding.

One essential aspect of communicating with your partner
is active listening. This involves fully focusing on what
your partner is saying without interrupting or judging,
and then reflecting back what you've heard to ensure
mutual understanding. Active listening creates a safe and

supportive space for both partners to express themselves without fear of judgment or criticism.

Another important aspect of communication is expressing your own thoughts, feelings, and needs openly and assertively. This requires vulnerability and courage, as you share your innermost thoughts and emotions with your partner. However, by expressing yourself authentically, you invite your partner into your inner world, fostering a deeper sense of intimacy and connection.

Conflict resolution is another crucial aspect of communication in relationships. Disagreements and conflicts are inevitable in any relationship, but how you navigate and resolve them can either strengthen or weaken your bond. Effective conflict resolution involves maintaining respect, empathy, and understanding towards your partner, even when you disagree. By approaching conflicts with a spirit of collaboration rather than competition, you can work together to find mutually satisfactory solutions that honor both partners' needs and feelings.

Intimacy Building Exercises

Intimacy-building exercises are practical activities and rituals designed to deepen the emotional, physical, and spiritual connection between partners. These exercises provide opportunities for partners to explore their desires, vulnerabilities, and fantasies in a safe and supportive environment, fostering a deeper sense of intimacy and trust.

One simple yet powerful intimacy-building exercise is the "love letter" exercise, where partners take turns writing heartfelt letters expressing their love, appreciation, and admiration for each other. This exercise allows partners to communicate their deepest feelings and desires in a vulnerable and authentic way, strengthening the emotional bond between them.

Another intimacy-building exercise is the "sensory exploration" exercise, where partners take turns exploring each other's bodies using their senses of touch, smell, and taste. This exercise promotes physical intimacy and arousal while deepening the emotional connection between partners.

Practicing mindfulness together is another effective intimacy-building exercise. Whether through meditation, yoga, or guided visualization, mindfulness practices allow partners to connect on a deeper level and cultivate a greater sense of presence and awareness in the relationship.

Finally, engaging in shared activities and experiences that bring joy and excitement, such as traveling, trying new hobbies, or exploring nature, can help partners create lasting memories and deepen their emotional connection.

Overall, rebuilding intimacy after heartbreak requires patience, compassion, and commitment from both partners. By reconnecting with yourself, communicating openly and honestly with your partner, and engaging in intimacy-building exercises, you can cultivate a relationship that is rich in love, trust, and intimacy.

Chapter 4

Restoring Self-Worth

Restoring self-worth after experiencing heartbreak is a transformative journey of self-discovery and self-compassion. Heartbreak can shatter one's sense of self-esteem and self-worth, leaving behind a trail of self-doubt and insecurity. In this chapter, I'll explore three essential components of restoring self-worth: challenging negative self-talk, building self-compassion, and setting boundaries.

Challenging Negative Self-Talk

Negative self-talk is the internal dialogue of self-criticism, doubt, and self-blame that can wreak havoc on one's self-esteem and self-worth. It's the voice that whispers, "You're not good enough," "You'll never find love again," or "It's all your fault." Challenging negative self-talk involves recognizing these harmful thought patterns and replacing them with more balanced and compassionate thoughts.

One effective strategy for challenging negative self-talk is cognitive restructuring, which involves identifying and reframing irrational beliefs and distorted thinking patterns. This may involve asking yourself questions such as, "Is this thought based on facts or assumptions?" "What evidence do I have to support or refute this belief?" and "What would I say to a friend who expressed similar thoughts and feelings?"

Additionally, practicing self-compassion is essential for challenging negative self-talk. Self-compassion involves treating oneself with kindness, understanding, and acceptance, especially in moments of struggle or failure.

Instead of berating yourself for perceived shortcomings or mistakes, offer yourself the same kindness and understanding you would offer to a loved one facing similar challenges.

Another helpful strategy for challenging negative self-talk is practicing mindfulness. Mindfulness involves observing your thoughts and emotions without attachment or judgment, allowing you to develop a greater sense of awareness and detachment from negative thought patterns. By practicing mindfulness, you can learn to recognize negative self-talk as passing mental phenomena rather than immutable truths about yourself.

Building Self-Compassion

Building self-compassion is essential for restoring self-worth and cultivating a deep sense of self-acceptance and self-love. Self-compassion involves recognizing your own humanity and treating yourself with kindness, understanding, and non-judgment, especially in moments of difficulty or failure. It's about offering yourself the same level of compassion and empathy you would offer to a close friend or loved one.

One powerful way to cultivate self-compassion is through self-care. Prioritizing your physical, emotional, and spiritual well-being through practices such as exercise, proper nutrition, adequate sleep, and relaxation techniques is crucial for replenishing your energy and fostering a sense of inner balance and harmony. By taking care of yourself, you signal to yourself and others that you are worthy of love, respect, and attention.

Another essential aspect of building self-compassion is practicing self-acceptance. Self-acceptance involves embracing all aspects of yourself, including your strengths, weaknesses, and imperfections, with kindness and understanding. Instead of striving for perfection or comparing yourself to unrealistic standards, practice accepting yourself exactly as you are in this moment, flaws and all.

Practicing gratitude is another powerful tool for cultivating self-compassion. Taking time each day to reflect on the things you're grateful for, no matter how small, can help shift your focus from what's lacking in your life to what's already present and meaningful. Gratitude fosters a sense of abundance and contentment, reducing feelings of inadequacy and self-doubt.

Setting Boundaries

Setting boundaries is essential for restoring self-worth and protecting your emotional well-being after experiencing heartbreak. Boundaries are the physical, emotional, and psychological limits that define how you expect to be treated by others and how you will respond when those boundaries are crossed. Setting boundaries involves clearly communicating your needs, desires, and limits to others and enforcing them consistently.

One essential aspect of setting boundaries is recognizing your own needs and priorities. Take time to reflect on what's important to you and what you need to feel safe, respected, and valued in your relationships. Once you've identified your boundaries, communicate them clearly and assertively to others, without apology or guilt.

Another important aspect of setting boundaries is enforcing them consistently. This may involve saying no to requests or behaviors that violate your boundaries, speaking up when your boundaries are crossed, and taking action to protect your emotional well-being. Remember that setting boundaries is not selfish or mean; it's an essential act of self-care and self-respect.

Practicing assertive communication is crucial for setting and maintaining boundaries effectively. Assertive communication involves expressing your thoughts, feelings, and needs in a clear, direct, and respectful manner, without being passive or aggressive. By practicing assertive communication, you can communicate your boundaries with confidence and clarity, reducing the likelihood of misunderstandings or conflicts.

Overall, restoring self-worth after heartbreak requires compassion, courage, and self-awareness. By challenging negative self-talk, cultivating self-compassion, and setting boundaries, you can reclaim your sense of self-worth and embrace your inherent value and worthiness. Remember that you are deserving of love, respect, and happiness, both from yourself and from others.

Chapter 5

Moving Forward with Hope and Confidence

Moving forward with hope and confidence after experiencing heartbreak is a courageous and transformative journey of self-discovery and personal growth. It's about finding the strength to rise above adversity, reclaiming your sense of agency and purpose, and embracing the possibilities that lie ahead. In this chapter, I'll explore three essential components of moving forward with hope and confidence: setting goals for the future, cultivating resilience, and finding meaning in your experience.

Setting Goals for the Future

Setting goals for the future is an empowering and forward-thinking process that allows you to envision the life you want to create for yourself beyond heartbreak. Goals provide direction, motivation, and a sense of purpose, guiding your actions and decisions as you navigate the challenges and opportunities of life.

When setting goals for the future, it's essential to start by clarifying your values, passions, and priorities. Reflect on what's truly important to you and what you aspire to achieve in various areas of your life, such as career, relationships, personal growth, and health. Use this self-reflection as a foundation for setting specific, measurable, achievable, relevant, and time-bound (SMART) goals that align with your values and aspirations.

Breaking down your goals into smaller, actionable steps can help make them more manageable and achievable. Create a plan of action outlining the specific steps you need to take to reach each goal, along with deadlines and milestones to track your progress. By breaking your goals down into bite-sized chunks, you can overcome feelings of overwhelm and inertia and make steady progress towards your aspirations.

It's also essential to remain flexible and adaptable in your goal-setting process, recognizing that life is inherently unpredictable and that circumstances may change along the way. Be open to reassessing and adjusting your goals as needed in response to new opportunities, challenges, and insights that arise along your journey.

Cultivating Resilience

Cultivating resilience is essential for navigating the inevitable ups and downs of life with grace, strength, and perseverance. Resilience is the ability to bounce back from adversity, adapt to change, and thrive in the face of challenges. It's about embracing setbacks as opportunities for growth and learning, rather than allowing them to define or defeat you.

One key component of resilience is developing a growth mindset, which involves viewing challenges and failures as opportunities for learning and growth, rather than fixed indicators of your abilities or worth. Embrace setbacks as valuable learning experiences that can help you develop new skills, perspectives, and strengths, rather than as reflections of your inherent inadequacy or failure.

Building a strong support network is another essential aspect of cultivating resilience. Surround yourself with supportive friends, family members, mentors, and professionals who can provide encouragement, guidance, and practical assistance during challenging times. Lean on your support network for emotional support, validation, and perspective, and don't hesitate to reach out for help when needed.

Practicing self-care is crucial for nurturing resilience and maintaining your physical, emotional, and spiritual well-being during times of stress and adversity. Prioritize activities that replenish your energy and foster a sense of inner balance and harmony, such as exercise, relaxation techniques, hobbies, and spending time in nature. By taking care of yourself, you can replenish your reserves and build the strength and resilience needed to navigate life's challenges with grace and fortitude.

Finding Meaning in Your Experience

Finding meaning in your experience of heartbreak is a transformative process that involves reflecting on the lessons learned, the growth achieved, and the personal strengths discovered along the way. It's about reframing your perspective from one of victimhood to one of empowerment, recognizing that even the most painful experiences can be catalysts for profound personal growth and transformation.

One powerful way to find meaning in your experience is through self-reflection and introspection. Take time to reflect on the lessons learned from your experience of heartbreak, the ways in which you've grown and changed as a result, and the personal strengths and qualities that have emerged or been strengthened through adversity. Use this self-reflection as a source of inspiration and motivation as you move forward with hope and confidence.

Engaging in acts of kindness and service can also help you find meaning in your experience by shifting your focus from your own pain and suffering to the needs of others. Volunteer work, acts of generosity, and random acts of kindness can provide a sense of purpose and fulfillment, while also fostering connections with others and contributing to the greater good.

Practicing gratitude is another powerful tool for finding meaning in your experience. Take time each day to reflect on the things you're grateful for, no matter how small, and express gratitude for the blessings and opportunities in your life. Gratitude fosters a sense of abundance and appreciation, reducing feelings of bitterness and resentment and promoting emotional well-being.

Moving forward with hope and confidence after experiencing heartbreak is a courageous and transformative journey of self-discovery and personal growth. By setting goals for the future, cultivating resilience, and finding meaning in your experience, you can reclaim your sense of agency and purpose, embrace the possibilities that lie ahead, and create a life filled with hope, resilience, and fulfillment.

Conclusion

Final Words of Encouragement

As I reach the conclusion of this journey from heartbreak to healing, it's essential to acknowledge the courage, resilience, and strength you've demonstrated along the way. Navigating the complexities of heartbreak is not easy, and yet here you are, standing tall and moving forward with hope and confidence. As you continue on your path of healing and self-discovery, remember that you are not alone. There is a vast community of individuals who have walked this path before you and who stand ready to offer support, guidance, and encouragement as you continue on your journey.

Embrace the lessons learned from your experience of heartbreak as valuable opportunities for growth and transformation. Each setback, each challenge, and each moment of pain has the potential to become a catalyst for profound personal growth and insight. Embrace the journey of self-discovery with an open heart and a willingness to learn from every experience, both positive and negative.

As you move forward with hope and confidence, remember to be gentle with yourself. Healing is not a linear process, and there will inevitably be setbacks and challenges along the way. Be patient with yourself and allow yourself the time and space to heal at your own pace. Celebrate your victories, no matter how small, and acknowledge the progress you've made, even when it feels insignificant.

Above all, remember that you are worthy of love, happiness, and fulfillment, just as you are. You are not defined by your past experiences or your perceived shortcomings. You are a resilient, courageous, and inherently valuable individual with limitless potential. Trust in your ability to overcome adversity, to navigate life's challenges with grace and resilience, and to create a life filled with meaning, purpose, and joy.

As you continue on your journey of healing and self-discovery, may you find the strength to embrace your vulnerability, the courage to face your fears, and the wisdom to listen to the whispers of your heart. May you cultivate deep and meaningful connections with yourself and others, and may you embrace the fullness of life with open arms and an open heart.

In closing, remember that the journey from heartbreak to healing is not just about overcoming pain and adversity; it's about embracing the fullness of life and rediscovering the inherent beauty and resilience within yourself. You are stronger, wiser, and more resilient than you realize, and you have the power to create a life filled with love, joy, and fulfillment. Keep moving forward with hope and confidence, knowing that brighter days lie ahead. You've got this.